THOMAS HARDY LISTENS TO LOUIS ARMSTRONG

THOMAS HARDY LISTENS

TO ANDREW LOUIS SHIELDS

ARMSTRONG

EYEWEAR PUBLISHING

First published in 2015
by Eyewear Publishing Ltd
74 Leith Mansions, Grantully Road
London W9 1LJ
United Kingdom

Typeset with graphic design by Edwin Smet
Author photograph Benno Hunziker
Printed in England by TJ International Ltd, Padstow, Cornwall

ISBN 978-1-908998-44-6

Eyewear wishes to thank Jonathan Wonham for his very generous patronage of our press;
as well as our other patrons and investors who wish to remain anonymous.

WWW.EYEWEARPUBLISHING.COM

ANDREW SHIELDS
lives with his wife and three children
in Basel, Switzerland, where he has been teaching at the
English Department at the University of Basel since 1995.
Cabinet d'Amateur (Cologne, Germany, 2005), a bilingual
pamphlet of poems with German translations by Ulrike
Draesner, appeared in 2005; his band Human Shields
released their debut CD, *Somebody's Hometown*, in 2015.
His translations from the German include works by Martin
Heidegger, Hannah Arendt, Durs Grünbein, and two
selections of the poetry of Dieter M. Gräf,
Tousled Beauty and *Tussi Research*, both
published by Green Integer.

Table of Contents

Hatter — 9
Static — 11
Records — 12
Monk's Dream — 13
Yorick Sings — 14
The Last D'Athée's Complaint — 15
Nuthatch — 16
Surf Scoter — 17
Land Without Nightingales — 18
Expat — 19
Hay Fever — 20
January Sixth — 22
Lace — 24
Eagle (Letter From My Aunt) — 25
There — 26
Sundowning — 27
Catalogue — 28
Son's Face — 30
Happening — 32
Aftermath — 33
Your Mileage May Vary — 34
Circus Elephant — 36
Better Never Than Late — 39
Edge — 41
Pipe Smoke — 42
He Who Hesitates — 44
Placebo — 45
The Seven-Year-Old Atheist — 46
The Circle Maker — 47
Highs In The Low Seventies — 48
Final Exam — 49
The Morning After The Night Before — 50
A Run — 51
Spring In My Step — 53

Feature Film — 54
Forsythia — 55
The Seating Plan — 56
Hic Sunt Leones — 58
Nostalgia — 59
Guitar — 60
Jehosaphat — 61
Tango — 62
Grateful Dead Concert — 64
Busker — 65
Someone — 66
Dirty Hands — 67
Long Enough — 69
Schism — 70
Pale Horse — 71
Green Man — 72
Tambourine — 73
Blackbird — 74
Without A Lyre — 75
Louisiana — 76
Ars Conjectandi — 78
Flugelhorn — 81
Thomas Hardy Listens To Louis Armstrong — 82
Verses — 84

Notes — 86
Acknowledgements — 88
Thanks — 89

Hatter

He plays the alto sax as if he's Bird;
he plays the tenor like a son of Trane.
He plays piano like a fan of Fats
or Count or Duke, those jazz aristocrats.
He's the Prince of Tides, the Jack of Hearts,
the Mary Poppins of his post-post-age.
He's the exterminated King of Rats.
He's a Queen surrounded by her cats.
He's the piper at the gates of dawn,
the drummer in the carnival parade.
He's a Princess with a bunch of brats.
He's a man of many hats.

He's a raincoat hanging up to dry,
an umbrella dripping in the tub.
He's all the boots left standing on the mats.
He cannot stop adjusting thermostats.
He's a hanger-out in smoke-free bars,
a picker-up of bills and girls and boys.
He's a frequenter of laundromats.
He's a murderer of diplomats.
He's a weatherman who never knows
which way the wind is blowing, or how hard.
He's the bane of faceless bureaucrats.
He's a man of many hats.

He's a spinster sewing for her nephews,
a sister who forgets her brother's birthday.
He's a teenage boy who always knows
what to say and where to put his hands.
He's a freshman checking out the frats.
He's a rookie choosing from his bats.
He's the ticket that will get you in.
He's a lion tamer with no lions,

a trapeze artist with a broken net.
He's a clown who never sheds a tear.
He's a juggler of acrobats.
He's a zebra being bugged by gnats.
He's an Egyptian plover flying down
to clean and floss a crocodile's teeth.
He's a pilotfish no shark will eat,
a parasite on some endangered crab.
He's a bird with many habitats.
He's the beer that's brewing in the vats,
the pesticide the vintners overuse.
He's an organic apple free of worms.
He's a sip of fine champagne, the cork
that flies across the room into your ear.
He's an on-line doctor with connections,
a salesman who can sell you anything.
He's a buyer with no caveats.
He is a man of many hats.

Static

I'm sitting in my in-laws' converted attic,
the cramped desk by the window covered with paper,
with line variations playing across each page
to unwritten melodies, and radio static

suddenly comes pouring down through the roof
between bursts of furious birdsong and takes
me back to the late-night sound of blue-white waves
broadcast from the Pacific to my room,

or to the moment when the car goes out
of range of one station before it is in range
of the next, so Creedence and Beatles play
through flurries of whitest noise, and then night shouts

for us to stop, if only for the stars
out here between the cities, far from day,
with only a radio to keep us awake,
and for an hour there've been no other cars,

or to my dawn whisper being the one
someone makes out through crackle, a student DJ
spinning something slow by Miles and Trane,
'All Blues' for the blue brought by the rising sun

to a sky as clear as Bill Evans' piano part
that plays in my head as I sit here in the attic,
forgetting my unfinished poems in radio static –
but no, it is the art of the black redstart.

Records

She walked high-school hallways, speaking
German learned from records
with her friends, their words a circling of secrets
from the others turning in their footsteps' echoes.

Now, her classes long past, the needle sticks.
In Kassel, her son interprets. Only when he's gone
does her scratchy German spin, but the stylus lifts
at his return, leaving her with English alone.

Monk's Dream

for Brad Mehldau

How many motes are drifting through the air?
(More than two hands would still not count them all.)
In the echoes of steps in long stone halls,
they play their waltzes and rondeaus, their airs
and songs of love, on instruments of glass
and light. O unrequited dust! (He stands
in the moonlight and listens, with both hands,
while dust and echoes settle, to the last
fading sounds he can hear, and the first sounds
he can't. He only moves again at dawn,
his only consolation now the thought
of someone somewhere else who hears the sounds
of motes and tries to count them, or someone long
ago, another dreamer at a loss.)

Yorick Sings

for Robin Höher

Good morrow, my sweet lord! How dost thou? My dust
returns your greeting from my doomsday's house.
Just as I mark your love, warn you I must:
questing crowners will soon dissect the laws

of all your pregnant problems and infinite jests.
Mark my words, as they will mark yours, my lord:
your lips, like those you kissed, when no more flesh,
will have no more matter than all your words.

'Gainst that, my lord, let us recall the hours
in which I bore you young upon my back,
and I will mock my grinning, mocking yours,
and from clown's grave with my clown's witting match

with each of your curious considerations
a card of absolute equivocation.

The Last D'Athée's Complaint

The Charter forbade me my due: the reputation
I might have established in royal service denied
because of my ancestors' crimes – unspecified
offenses to the safety of the nation.

So I refuse to bow before a King
who insists he must withhold the reason,
from those who suffer in his state, why treason
condemns not just a traitor but his offspring

and every generation still to come.
I shall not give a child to this land
that starved my fathers though they bit no hand.
To argument, like him, I'm deaf and dumb.

He gladly suffers fools who form the rings
of hell around him, but I don't suffer Kings.

Nuthatch

The paper's in the tree whose trunk is split,
the one the nuthatch will be climbing down.
The words I was afraid to write on it
will tell you where to go. Be there at dawn.

You'll find the matches by another tree.
Burn the paper. If the smoke drifts west,
you've arrived. Sit down and wait for me.
I'll come from the east when the new moon sets.

But if the smoke drifts elsewhere, or the paper
doesn't burn, then I have gone my way
already. I'll have left you bread and water.
Eat. Drink. Do not sit down. Do not wait.

I won't return. I will not bid you read
the scars the nuthatch pecked into the bark,
revealing where I went to disappear
in the language of the meadowlark.

Surf Scoter

To be a surf scoter parting the water,
orange bill, white nape, and black tail
recklessly leaving the rocks alone

with the breakers and a belted kingfisher.
To lean too far and find out what it is
to fly, the air pouring out of my ears.

To race, and never cross the finish line,
winds uncounted after the second,
each breath burning with ease. To steal

myself, putting the goods in the myriad pockets
of a long wool coat worn by a crestfallen man
whose nine-day beard is dappled with gray,

nothing but humbug and time in his hands
while his fingers dream of fingering
what's on the discount shelves. To disconnect

the telephone, the ten thousand numbers
I dialed forgotten. To wake up and find myself
gone, the sheets still twisted and warm,

my winter socks left behind. To wait outside
a window, then depart before you open
the shutters on another dawn.

Land Without Nightingales

A sparrow grew up to the moon;
tailfeathers clouded the sky.
A panda inherited noon;
April came into the light.

> The land without nightingales slept
> and woke to the mockingbird's song.
> The judge in the one-way street wept
> and put off her ruling till dawn.

The marriage of blackbird and thrush
shattered the hopes of the finch.
She threw her bouquet with a blush,
then woke from her dream with a pinch.

> The land without nightingales slept
> and woke to the mockingbird's song.
> The judge in the one-way street wept
> and put off her ruling till dawn.

The storks in the trees at the zoo
are wild but migrate no more.
They clatter the whole winter through
and feed where the cold water's warm.

> The land without mockingbirds slept
> and woke to the nightingale's song.
> The judge in the one-way street left;
> she'd put off her ruling too long.

Expat

The barstool's capacious, then ever more enclosed,
with every beer, as evening erodes.

A few capricious tourists off the cozy track
propose unbeaten toasts. He'll soon be going back.

Mannequin musicians play mandolins or thumb pianos,
bleat out a reggae air on ragged banjos.

The booths patter with the local lingo.
Smattered English polishes the windows.

An amble to the john, the mirror's random crack.
The urinal's askew. He'll soon be going back.

The minimal solicitudes of seven-minute flirts:
blurted-out soliloquies, well-trained parting words.

Insert pejorative for natives here,
before a sputtered call for one more beer.

Dusty carnations; carnival bric-a-brac –
long-faded revelations. He'll soon be going back.

Hay Fever

for Joachim Sartorius

The Belgian pharmacist's assistant
broke her trying English through
my breaking French, my mind a mist
of pollen and Benadryl: 'For you,

this drug.' It meant the end of eyes
flooded like gutters, of the song
of unceasing sneezes, of lying
thick with sleep the whole day long.

O Hismanol! O drug of choice
in chestnut May when everything
begins to bloom – except my voice
in foreign languages. Each spring

I bought a pack, until a German
allergist almost put an end
to years of easy breaths: 'O sure,
it works, but I am not a friend

of Hismanol.' O side effects
beyond my powers of description
in any language! O dejection!
But he penned a new prescription:

O fluent Zyrtec! Keep the German
and the French I memorized
by turning flashcards from returning
to *Nichts, néant*, nothing, lies;

keep all those conjugations from
evaporating in the haze
of pollen. But when the dog days come,
not even Zyrtec has its way,

and then I pray for air to breathe,
for words my lips can form around.
O sleep! O god of speech! Relieve
my tongue, and tongues, with a round
of rain: the only lovely sound
in this monolingual season.

January Sixth

Johnny's in the attic now, and the snow
has started to cover the skylight with the slightest
sound disappearing into silence.
A bare bulb shines on an unlabeled box –
a set of Pyrex tubes. He pulls one out,
looks through the still clean glass at all the dust
he's stirred up by digging around up here,
seeking nothing in particular
but whatever feeling he might find.

The air begins to summon back the Christmas
cough that laid him up till New Year's Day.
He pulls up the cord behind his Bauhaus lamp;
out comes a badge that someone must have worn
since he was a kid – or just held up
to the light to see one corner of the star
had broken off. And on the wall is Bogart –
what's the use of a man in a fedora
no one ever smiles to recall?
He used to dream of repartee, of friendships
that were beautiful enough to end.

There's a paisley cloth on Dad's old trunk,
and the lid only opens with a slippery effort
and a cut on his knuckle. Sucking a trace of blood,
he fingers a pair of old sandals it made
no sense to keep, all sentiment forgotten.
This dug-up life just barely feels like his.
Here's a set of guitar strings for the guitar
he'd never seriously played, then handed on
to Bob, who went off overseas and wrote
so many letters, all so long he never
read them, sending only postcards back.

When had he last recalled this model airplane?
In the basement, when he should've been in bed,
he'd slowly glued the balsa, piece by piece.
The smell of the glue had slowly overwhelmed
the smell of the wood; he'd gotten dizzy with it
and his lack of sleep, but kept on building.
It'd flown so often, breaking only once,
a simple enough repair – will it fly again?
He's a man in an attic shuffling through his stuff,
things forgotten, things he'll never remember;
he's throwing away his life while the snow falls
and the wind blows whichever way it blows.

Lace

To our reflections
the tiny border or rim of
her world is red now.
In their inside-out coats, they run
through the octaves of all
the scales in all the keys,
open their scores to discover
roses, roses, roses.
We ponder what she must be
thinking: where there is red,
no pew is empty after they
fall to pieces. She is not
a precious metal – when you
remove the lace she wears,
the core of her self is tin, nothing
but a letter.

Eagle (Letter From My Aunt)

for Barbara Robbins

It's been sitting there an hour, watching
huge flocks of ducks in sunrise.

I saw a pair come in, but now
there's only the one in the tree.

How can I go out to do laundry
without disturbing it?

Two deer went through the yard
last night when we weren't peeking.

Their tracks surround the bird feeder,
though it's empty. Time for a refill.

We expect cold for a few more days,
watching ice form along the shoreline.

For generations, the neighbours have kept
a log of when the ice breaks up in spring.

I suppose their log tells them
when it closes over the lake, too.

Last winter was so hard on deer the hunters
are cancelling their rooms. Why bother?

Dan saw fresh antler-rub marks yesterday.
Not many tracks, should've been more.

He's bundled up for work, but
trying to get a picture first.

I better go watch, in case
it soars off again.

There

When I was there, all the people were talking
Italian. I made my way down the nine long flights.
Everyone was trying to get to the bar.
I didn't stand a chance – and I needed a drink.
'The terrible thing', the band kept singing and singing,
'is when you're there, you can't even tell.'
I wanted to pay my respects to our famous host,
who never deigns to rise to greet his guests,
but I couldn't find him for the crowd.
When I finally slipped through a side door,
I found myself at the edge of a frozen pond.
'Mom!' I cried, without the slightest idea
as to why, 'Dad!' I stepped onto the ice,
calling – 'Mom! Dad!' – while walking toward the stars.

Sundowning

The chickens are back in their coop.
The kids are out on the town.
It's here in one fell swoop.
    It's sundown.

You've heard them say it before.
The rumour's been going around.
You're heading straight for the door.
    It's sundown.

    You've forgotten what you said.
    All that matters is here and now.
    No one's getting you to bed,
    even though it's sundown.

The trucks roll by on the highway.
You want to follow that sound.
You want to have your say
    at sundown.

The dusk turns into dark.
You walk away with a frown.
You're the only one in the park
    past sundown.

    Here's where the children played,
    but they're not here right now.
    You don't want to end your day,
    even though it's sundown.

Catalogue

As always, the story begins with another.

Imagine a librarian cataloguing slides,
her fingers so familiar with their edges.
Here is the white peacock, here the holy family
behind an open curtain. Here is a cat
under a table; here are two boys singing.
Each painting lives beyond the walls
it hangs on – lives, here, with its number,
in a box, in a drawer. The gargoyles
are filed under architecture. Imagine
how the carvers bent to the stone,
how the painters faced the canvas,
how the cataloguer holds each image
up to the light and finds its rightful place.

Imagine the woman standing on the corner
of two Brazilian streets, so young in the heat
of the nineteen fifties. This is
not Michigan; this is what Michigan would be
to those born here. She's been borne this far –
her whole life before her, her whole life
behind her, in her, all around her,
unimaginable. Remember
when you were somewhere,
somewhere you had never been before?
She's been borne this far – metaphors
always go farther. The Arctic tern
migrates between polar summers. She'll go
beyond the erratics of Ann Arbor, and return.
Imagine the woman passing a house
she lived in as a child. It's summer.
The Washtenaw Dairy's open at the end of the street,
a single scoop in a cup instead of a double cone.

Remember when you were somewhere
you had been before? It's time to tell
her daughter-in-law the buttermilk story.
Hot with play, she left the afternoon behind
and entered the cool air of the kitchen.
Picture the one you grew up in, the counter,
the tall, cold glass. She took a swig
and spat out the unexpected buttermilk
just as her mother returned. Somewhere there's a kitchen
where you could leave your own glass
on the counter, come back to see your own daughter
spit out your buttermilk, as hers did.

Now the woman is reading a poem
at night. Perhaps she knows the poet,
and his voice covers the few sounds
coming in from the dark. She's known
that voice as long as it has spoken. She heard
its first words; they were spoken to her.
She feels spoken to as she reads;
she finds herself in every line.
But as always, the story ends with another.
Your life has borne you here, in the tern's shadow.
There's a glass of something on the counter.
Are you bent to the page? Look up
at the canvas, hold the slide
up to the light, and see.

Son's Face

for Miles

Around your mouth is the trace
of a woman with a drawer
of sweets to choose from at
the end of every Sunday visit,
and another of a lumberjack
still tall at ninety, the trees he'd cut
all long since burned, or sent as stuff
for houses downstream to Superior.

Your brow's the wake of uncles: Martin,
lost in Siberia, a German prisoner
of war, his sister and her baby daughter
also lost in late-war fire-bombing.
Dudley was ill in wartime England,
where he met his second wife, a nurse
(his first refused to give him a divorce –
then killed herself instead).

This furrow is a Hessian farmer
made a cripple by the war
before. The village treasurer, he'd walk
on his two canes to meet the mail truck
and take the taxes into town, his brace
hidden under his trousers. Back home,
he'd sit in the kitchen with his youngest daughter,
cooking for the family in the fields.

At your temples, there are hints
of more ancient uncles,
two Union generals. A drunk
three times a Senator, the only man
to beat the Rebel Stonewall Jackson
in the field, James Shields left Ireland

years before the famine began.
The other was Oliver Otis Howard,
Indian expert, founder of colleges
for emancipated slaves
and poor white trash, pursuer,
despite misgivings, of the Nez Perce
on their flight to Canada.

The lines you don't have yet
come from Johan and Nicholas Handwerk,
two brothers who sailed from Rotterdam
for Philadelphia in 1739
on the *Loyal Judith*, while under them
may be a Huguenot fleeing
the bonfires of the Revocation
of the Edict of Nantes for
safe haven in Kassel, as well as two
who sailed to Plymouth once
to build a City on a Hill.

Happening

He stood up suddenly and threw
himself and his grey canvas sack
to the bus's floor, then, clutching
the sack's edges, he struck the floor
with it again, four or five times,
then stopped. No one moved, everyone
had moved for a moment, away
from him as he had struck the floor.

He sat looking at the contents
of the bag, now strewn all over.
Cassettes, broken cassette cases,
assorted papers, and pieces
of his old cassette recorder.
He sat quite still for a moment.
Whatever had been happening
wasn't happening anymore.

Nothing continued to happen,
then something began to happen
again. He began to pick up
his things, put them into the sack.
No one moved. They all looked at him,
or they all tried not to look at him.
He put his things into the sack
with steadily increasing speed.

Aftermath

Another journey underway,
the painter on the foredeck of
the overloaded ferryboat
sees, past the sea wall and out
over the straits, the aftermath
of sunlight from behind the clouds,
a brighter form of rain. The harbour
opposite moves from blur into focus
as the ferry moves, its wake
first spray in the painter's face.
Light and cloud and mist: what is
to be captured on canvas. He'll hold
the brush in the air the way the ship,
sailing without a sail, hangs
before it falls again down on
the waves. Behind him, every stroke
he's ever painted; the unpainted
before him, this passage from one harbor
to another, the ferry rolling,
with every breaker, deeper down
in what is, what will have been.

Your Mileage May Vary

1

Our last night in the house was not our last.
With two cats in the yard. The movers took
the furniture in the morning. *A country where
they turned back time.* Lifting a trunk, Dad felt
something slip in his back. *I have become
comfortably numb.* No driving with such pain.
The day destroys the night. Our real last night,
footsteps on hardwood floors. *People and friends
I still can recall.* Sean with his singles player.
Dream until your dream comes true. Dan,
an even match across the ping-pong table.
They're the faces of the stranger. A girlfriend
kissed in the sunroom. *She can take the dark
out of the nighttime.* Too shy or young for more.
I'm already standing on the ground.
Training for cross country with the other,
better runners. *Get up, get up, get out
of the door.* A twenty-mile summer
thunderstorm. *Into this world we're thrown.*
The melancholy of second place. *I've paid
my dues, time after time.* The dream the Red Sox
might someday win it all. *When I was young,
it seemed that life was so wonderful.*

2

Leaving in the morning with Dad in the back.
The danger on the rocks is surely past.
Big sisters with licenses. *Baby you can drive
my car.* One last trip West. *Running into
the sun.* Not down through the desert to Christmas
on a San Diego beach. *All the leaves
are brown.* Not down from the Rockies to speed
across Nevada. *Like endless rain into*

a paper cup. No stop in Medicine Bow,
highway hung on a ridge. *Mountains come
out of the sky.* No hummingbirds surrounding
my uncle's Colorado cabin. *Come
with me or go alone.* Instead we went
to North Dakota, then up to Winnipeg
to visit cousins. *Leave us helpless, helpless,
helpless.* The even more endless highways
of Canada. *Get your kicks.* In Glacier,
footsteps without sound, each breath clouding
another constellation. *Open up
your mind and float downstream.* Front-row seats
for the Red Sox in Seattle. *Sweet
little sixteen.* A foul ball that Dad
leapt up to grab. *Joltin' Joe has left
and gone away.* Going on to Palo Alto.
Be sure to wear some flowers in your hair.
Arriving on Labor Day, Grace Slick's concert
spilling into the new backyard. *One pill
makes you larger, and one pill makes you small.*
Our first night in the house, and not our last.
Johnny come lately, there's a new kid in town.

Circus Elephant

for Jane Holland

I was once a circus elephant
in Leamington Spa, but when I first set foot
in the Big Top of Sydenham School, the kids
ignored my trunk and demanded that I speak
American. The right words didn't cross
my pachydermic mind; instead of saying
'Deuteronomy' or 'ferkydoodle',
I stammered into speechlessness until
they pelted me with peanuts and made me play
goalie in their schoolyard football matches.
Without a trainer to tell me what to do
and give me treats for every job well done,
I just stood there with a puzzled look,
but I was so wide that no-one scored unless
they tunneled the ball between my sluggish legs,
so my team always won, and after a while,
I was never chosen last again.
In class, the teachers were unhappy with
my writing, but I found it hard to hold
the unfamiliar English fountain pens
without a lot of smudging, and anyway,
I had to learn to spell all over again.
One teacher raged about my scribbling
and how I didn't say 'sir' when I said 'yes';
he didn't recognize my well-trained bow
or offer me a treat to teach me right.
Invited for a sleepover by a friend,
I made the bathtub overflow and soaked
the hallway floor as well when I couldn't find
a towel that was close to big enough.
Another friend was kind enough to make
a date to play some football in his garden.
Asked to call on Sunday around half three,

I phoned to say that I'd be over soon,
which made him think I wasn't going to call.
When I finally made it to his house,
I managed not to trample all the grass
around his makeshift goal; he even switched
and let me try to score some goals for once,
but with my clumsy feet I couldn't score at all,
and it had been decided that my trunk
was like the other players' hands and arms,
the limb that I was not allowed to use
whenever I wasn't banished to the goal.
On Guy Fawkes Day, the crackers were too loud
for my acutely sensitive ears, and the fire
burned up so high I almost ran away.
But even louder was the reenactment
of the Siege of Warwick Castle, loud
enough that I remember nothing more
of all the Cavaliers and Roundheads but
the smoke with which their muskets filled the air.
And once the school went on a trip to France,
a half-term holiday in the *Massif Central*.
I schlepped myself in summer tennis shoes
through springtime snow up to a mountain top
from which we could see nothing through the fog,
with socks and shoes that didn't want to dry.
I started sniffing away the rest of the hols,
frightening the French with the fury of my sneezes.
I did not notice that I had forgotten
how to speak American; it seemed more like
it was the English who had started speaking
ever so much more clearly than before.
I squeezed myself into a Stratford playhouse
to hear the actors trained in Shakespeare strain
to sing the twangy drawls of *Oklahoma!*
and later heard my Michigan cousins struggling
the other way around with *Oliver*.
I'd become invisible in England,

just another schoolboy in his uniform
(though one with a funny nose and ears that made
those of the Prince of Wales seem ordinary).

An elephant in Leamington is forced
to teach himself so many clever tricks
that are useless in America,
where the only gig that I could find,
after nine months of football and dropped Rs,
was in an enclave for the upper crust,
a suburb where no circus elephants
were ever even asked to speak or bow.
The best thing that could happen was to be
ignored, but everybody turned to stare
at such a clumsy mastodon as me.
And if I raised my elephantine voice,
soon halfway British, halfway Midwest twang,
they all threw more than words and peanuts at me.
Sticks and stones and blows and names all hurt
the same. I'd creep back home and fill the tub
to spray myself and wash the cuts and scratches,
with nothing left to me of England but
my memories of saves when I was a goalie,
a circus elephant in Leamington.

Better Never Than Late

I was baptised twice, but still it didn't stick.
First, as a dying baby, I became a Catholic.
When I'd been saved from Limbo came my first heresy:
I was made a Protestant when I'd forgotten I'd been sick.
        Better never than late for me.

He put off his deathbed conversion until another day,
when all the broken promises will have been unmade
and wrapped up in a package with a pretty ribbon
just waiting for Pandora to come along and say,
        'Better never than late for him.'

When the spirit came to save her, she'd already left home
to turn one trick too many to feed her baby and her jones.
She heard that preacher's words as he turned away with a curse,
throwing down the money beside her unanswered cell phone,
        'Better never than late for her.'

You've heard a million voices, seen a thousand points of light,
but Jesus never comes to you on a backsliding night,
and salvation's just another tale for you to misconstrue
if nobody answers when you ask what's wrong or right,
        'Better never than late for you.'

Two fire engines scurry past; the sirens doppler down.
They speak in tongues in that storefront church and writhe
    down on the ground,
but the dealer in the back room chokes on smoke and phlegm
and rasps out when he sells his shit by the ounce or by the pound,   39
        'Better never than late for them.'

They wanted to be a big-city story, that was all,
so they called some number scratched on a bathroom wall.
The ringing at the other end sounded ominous,
and when it finally ended, one said, 'Don't make another call.
      Better never than late for us.'

Edge

Across the curving waters, far from home,
a park in the Old World, ice on the ground,
low winter clouds, each breath another cloud.
A dog, unleashed, crossing the field, alone
with what it's chasing, running back to find
its master's feet, the story of his hands
and roughly scratching fingers, of a land
to return to, an ordered world to mind,
complete with corner nook and bed beside
the hearth. Stand in the park, a Sargasso Sea,
a doldrums, watch the dogs and masters, be
still as a sail with no wind left inside,
wait until the cold says where to head,
a bed not in a home but still a bed,
though one so narrow fear lies at its edge,
as if the world were square and heaven whole,
the way to the New World blocked not by cold
but by the flat earth's limits, the park's hedge.
If Columbus underestimated
the true circumference of the earth, so that
he first found only water where he'd thought
to find the Indies (claiming even later
that was indeed what he had found), at least
America was there to rescue him.
The running dog, the winter on cold skin,
the sailors clamouring to turn back east,
no more wind blowing, Indies to the west,
a cloud across the heavens – just a breath.

Pipe Smoke

Grandpa died at the end of the war,
but not of the war. He died of the flu.
The flu took him when I was four,
took the finest smell I knew:

pipe smoke and whisky. Papa chose
cheap cigarettes and cheaper wine,
or they chose him. Where Grandpa rose
from nothing to whisky (every line

he put his money in was good),
everything that Papa tried
led back to wine: from coffin wood
and dimestore rings to fixing fights

and running bootleg gin. His sons
could see he couldn't hold his wine
like his father. His drinking done,
he'd come to beat us. Grandpa's pipe

lay on the mantelpiece unsmoked
until my elder brother stole
some pipe tobacco that he smoked
with our two cousins and me. We stole

out of the house one early morning
and made our way through town to where
we spent the years between the wars,
our childhood: the cemetery,

the family crypt, our Grandpa's grave.
Coughing, we dropped the pipe. It broke,
and then we four could not escape
a beating. The smell of the wine and the smoke

of cheap cigarettes erased the taste
of Grandpa's pipe. His taste for theft
awakened, my brother stole a case
of dusty bootleg gin still left

from my father's failure, too cheap
even for him to drink. We drank
the entire case, my father asleep
from a binge of his own. When he woke, we stank

of vomit and gin, and the beating that came
was the last we'd ever know:
rings had opened my brother's face
when I brought a bottle down

on my father's head. Who mourned
his death? My brother ran away
as soon as he saw him fall. I swore
at him for leaving me that day,

and to everyone else I swore
my brother'd done it. He never came
back home again. Before the war,
we met by chance once more, his face

still scarred. We drank, then drank some more –
whisky – drank as brothers do.
I heard he died at the end of the war,
but of the war, and not of the flu.

He Who Hesitates

There is a saint for doubt.
– Glyn Maxwell, 'Didymus the Seated'

As they broke the gate down, he turned around
to look for uncertain faces, and fell to the ground.
The crowd pushed forward over him, chanting the names
of death in every language that they knew.
For seconds on end, he took in the procession of shoes
and voices, till everything became the same.

> The boy at the end of the row is breathing still.
> He was covered by two bodies killed
> by the surge of people storming the gate.
> Their dying saved a boy they did not know.
> His glasses shattered around his broken nose.
> He's breathing, but he hardly has a face.

He remembers that he turned – but not why.
The gate had broken down, and with a sigh,
the crowd had been released into its rage.
Its pressure grew, then something in him broke:
the words in other mouths no longer spoke
through his, but tore and turned him like a page.

> The boy at the end of the row has shattered eyes
> that seem to speak about the truths and lies
> that led the raging crowd to charge that gate.
> The boy at the end of the row has lost his voice;
> his gaze has left his nurses with no choice:
> they write down what they think those eyes translate.

Placebo

Placebo Domino in regione vivorum
– (Psalm 116:9)

It's vespers for the dead,
humouring the quick.
It's comfort for the sick,
to keep away their dread.

The singers please the Lord
in the land of the quick.
Their tears are but a trick
played with a minor chord.

A little sugar pill
cuts no one to the quick.
The singing does the trick
for mourners and the ill.

The Seven-Year-Old Atheist

The universe gives me the creeps.
– Willem de Kooning

The seven-year-old atheist knew the sky
of California, in winter even bluer
than in summer. He knew that cats could die,
like grass beneath a stone, and children, too.

With his every breath, the universe
expanded, made him smaller. So he willed
himself to grow, energetically cursed –
'God damn it to hell!'– his puny build.

Neither curse nor prayer could change the speed
of light or turn his energy to mass.
He did not breathe in vain. He did not need
mysterious ways. He lay down on the grass

and dreamed he was a stone that someone kicked.
He would have been surprised at his own trick,
if he had disappeared. Instead, he flew
across the lawn, then landed, woke, and grew.

The Circle Maker

The circle I draw around myself
can only be seen by me.
I draw it every day at twelve
wherever I happen to be.

My noontide shadow is so small;
it cowers close to me.
By evening, it's proud and tall
out toward infinity.

If once my ring was a demand
for rain to wash away
the dust of drought throughout the land,
I now have nought to say.

Wherever I am, my circle is;
my shadow travels far.
The fame is mine; the world is his.
I sing to my guitar.

The song forgets the circle's there
and says I'm free to go,
as if I could wake up somewhere
far from all I know,

or I could sleep for seventy years
and find myself a name
whose living voice nobody hears
despite my lasting fame.

I dream of drawing everything –
a boat, a bird, a saint –
but my shadow and my ring
are all that I can paint.

Highs In The Low Seventies

The summer's weather waits on the Atlantic,
a puffin's wingbeat making all the difference,
or none, between a board game and a picnic
some August afternoon. The year's first swifts
come curving out of the late April dusk;
they'll go back to Africa before
that choice is made, between rain and risk,
between sun and thunder. The shutting of a door,

a moment's pause to listen to a bird
singing out of sight, is enough to decide.
Time hovers like a kestrel or a tern;
I hover, but I do not strike: I ride
the seasons like a buoy the ocean rings:
Here's shallow water. The puffin folds its wings.

Final Exam

Thirty-seven heads bend over paper
while thirty-seven hands scrawl hectic text.
The sprawl of pages on the tables covers
the spreading fear of being incorrect.

One by one, the students raise their eyes
to see which cracking beam might have the answers,
or squint out through the windows for the hints
the courtyard trees have hidden in their branches.

The sparrows speak of sparrow things; the water
sounding in the fountain cannot say
what's wrong or right. But still the students look
everywhere for help but at their papers.

If they see me following their gazes,
they turn back, with small, embarrassed smiles,
to the tables' scratched and varnished grain,
as if knowledge might be in such lines.

But perhaps the answers *can* be had
from all this dead and living wood, the beams
and furniture that listen to the lectures,
the growing trees that drink the light with leaves.

Outside, the breeze abates; the trees grow still.
A chaffinch chants a final song, a swift
screes off, and now there's no sound but the fountain
to tell the students how much time is left.

The Morning After The Night Before

Your breathing fogs the early winter air.
The bus will come when the time is right.
A voice in your head is singing, 'There, there.'
What were you thinking last night?

The dry leaves scatter all around your feet.
Another morning comes with later light.
The voice is singing against the beat.
What were you thinking last night?

The sun's too weak to make a proper blue.
Your socks are dirty, your pants too tight.
The singer cannot tell you what to do.
What were you thinking last night?

If clouds could talk, they'd laugh about your dreams.
Your aching eyes make everything too bright.
Each song is never more than what it seems.
What were you thinking last night?

Is this morning one that you'll remember?
Or one you should forget with all your might?
Has the singing ever been so tender?
What were you thinking last night?

A Run

Down my most tangled paths of reverie
A man with a transistor radio walks.
– Daniel Hoffman, 'O Sweet Woods'

We drove to the park to go for a run,
       my wife, her father, and I.
A five-kilometer loop through woods
       down paths that weren't quite dry.

We didn't say a word. I ran
       with thoughts at first, or rather
fragments of them, then memories
       of longer runs with my own father,

from laughing talk to the steady silence
       I so rarely find.
Inside the pounding of our feet,
       there was nothing in my mind.

       ★

I ran ahead to the parking lot,
       where picnickers had turned
the volume on their radio up.
       'Blue Bayou' would have burned

its tune into my emptied head
       if I had not stayed
by the exit, far from them,
       far from our car, to wait

until the two I'd left behind
       had stretched, and fetched the car.
They drove over to pick me up
       where I was standing as far

from music as I ever would.
        The din that fills my brain I'd run
away from, and then my father-in-law
        turned the radio on.

Spring In My Step

The summer never ended
until I got some payment for my pains
  that helped me get through autumn
despite October and November rains
  turning into winter snow
so that I had to put on the damn chains.
  Now there's a spring in my step,
  but I still need some coffee in my veins.

  Though I've loved a few women,
I'm tired of all these Janes and Elaines.
  I would have let them all be
if I were somebody with any brains.
  Now I'm leaving them behind;
I'll steal a couple aeroplanes and trains.
  I've got a spring in my step,
  but I still need some coffee in my veins.

  Am I really in the red?
I have to add up my losses and gains.
  Here's my favourite hourglass;
I'm counting and recounting all the grains.
  I'm pondering everything
everybody who's anybody feigns.
  I've got a spring in my step,
  but I still need some coffee in my veins.

  I'm waiting for the new moon;
I'll leave when it waxes, not when it wanes.
  I'll head straight down the road;
you'll never catch me changing lanes.
  I'll head out to the Rockies,
driving right across the Great Plains.
  I've got a spring in my step,
  but I still need some coffee in my veins.

Feature Film

Last night, I dreamed another feature film.
Its celluloid has faded and decayed
so only disconnected scenes remain,
hand-held pans of landscapes and grainy stills

of minor characters with trademark smiles
displaced by grimaces. The title song,
a bleat of pop my ear snatched up along
the river, or something sung by my son Miles,

never ceases to repeat its theme
without a variation. Every take
lost at the final cut is a phantom ache
that harries me beyond the final scene.

Forsythia

A golden explosion
        of forsythia
                keeps my eye
                        off the band,

but a hedgehog is listening
        beside a mushroom
                it's forgotten to eat
                        to the tiny musicians

in their little red hats.
        I have to pretend
                to be able to hear
                        the song they're playing,

but I can see
        the yellow flowers
                making a music
                        of their own.

The Seating Plan

At six, the party started, but not till eight
was dinner served. Everyone was dressed
a shade too formally and drank the wait
away with two drinks more than what was best.

A few, then far too many, stood between
the tables and the stage, their eyes on chairs
they sought their names on. More than being seen
was seeing who was graceful, who had airs

of being chosen for the places near
the host, his family, and his entourage.
They mingled, chatted, tried to hide their fear,
until a little man came on the stage,

picked up a knife, and tapped a glass three times.
'If you would take your seats, we can begin.'
By every setting lay some rhyming lines
that were supposed to make their readers grin.

They wandered drunkenly around the hall,
reciting mangled versions of those verses,
until the words meant nothing more at all
and they could not tell their blessings from their curses.

When finally everyone just took a seat
and made their places' rhymes into their own,
no little man came out to carve the meat,
nor did the host sit down up on his throne.

That's when a young man thought to try the door
and found it was a painted bas relief.
The windows were all murals, nothing more,
quite worthy of suspended disbelief.

Imaginary cities waited there,
and everyone could find themselves in one,
all dressed just as they were, without a care,
all heading home, the lavish banquet done.

Hic Sunt Leones

At the Basel Zoo

The fence around the building site was gone;
the lions' habitat was finally done.
I could not see them. The big cats needed time
to adapt to their new home, explained a sign.

Coming back months later, I spotted the pride
between two bushes, no longer needing to hide.
The lioness began to growl, then roared
and charged at someone right behind the wall.
She stopped a second later, looking bored,
the zoo still echoing with her stifled call.

Nostalgia

In the dream of the chough and its call so close to your ear,
        you wash your hands and leave the mountain behind.
        You stand by the river where the word was coined
and drop it in where the water's a little less clear.

When you get on the train, there's someone else in your seat,
        a boy who looks at you as if he knows.
        There's someone in the background wherever you go
who also heard that call, and felt the wingbeat.

Guitar

The guitar in the corner sings when you sing,
and keeps on singing when you stop.
Even after dark, it rings and rings,
quieter than each pin you drop.

Just when it seems that's all,
the telephone rings
and makes it weep until another call –
the blackbird's – makes it sing.

Jehosaphat

Jehosaphat let the singers sing;
      his foes turned on his foes.
He climbed a tower in the wild
      and scattered all the crows.

The magpies joined them in the field,
      collecting jewels and gold,
the shiny things that people love,
      from bodies grown cold.

Jehosaphat let trumpets play,
      and harps and psalteries,
while all the crows and magpies flew
      back up into the trees.

Tango

While the band is tuning up,
        the singer lurks offstage
and eyes the dancers nursing drinks.
        They don't look half her age.

The old bandoneonist picks
        an older melody.
The young one tries to find the chords;
        the bassist finds the key.

The singer steps out on the stage;
        the dancers take the floor
to go through all the motions that
        they've gone through before.

But in the shining spot, the singer
        can't help but hesitate.
She rushes to the microphone
        but still comes in too late.

The band plays on as if that were
        how she had meant to sing.
And while she lags behind the beat,
        the dancers do their thing.

The verses and the chorus sung,
        she slips out of the light
and off the stage, and out the door
        into the silent night.

The band plays on; the dancers dance
        as if the melody
does not need words to be a song
        but just a minor key.

And when the song comes to an end,
     there's still so much applause,
as if the singer were still there
     to take her well-earned bows.

Grateful Dead Concert

sometime in the nineteen-eighties

I bought a tie-dye T-shirt from a vendor
outside the venue. The band began to play
just as the dose kicked in, six musicians sent
to be my guides. Some girl spinning in the hallway
was dancing with me – one song might tell me where.
The crowd parted like water, or like air,
and the eyes of the strangers opened and opened, wide.

With all our seeking, we were nowhere. Outside,
the rain had left behind a crescent moon,
singing us a rare, indifferent tune.

Busker

The violinist on the bridge is playing
a minor melody with rich vibrato
that every passing bus and tram drowns out.

The fragments of the tune drift down the river,
reminding all the passersby of songs
whose words have long been drowned out by the years.

Someone

Someone's singing in the train.
Light leaps against the window.
The two people I can see
are looking at their hands.

The singer breaks off, leaving
the sound of the air
and the tracks. I can see
someone in the dark glass.

Dirty Hands

for Antje Majewski's triptych 'Schmutzige Hände'

1

Who's looking at you? Who's looking at you? The sun
is casting shadows on the platform: yours,
and those of the pole you lean on and the bar
the pole supports. The metal's warm, so bitter
against your palm. You brush hair and sweat
from your forehead. Who's looking at you? Your sister
is looking past you down the platform, she
cannot see the train. The platform's tiles,
the shadows of the pole, the bar, and you;
your sister's shadow, the platform's edge – a camera
is looking at you, a lens; a painter's looking
at the photograph. The painting's printed
in a catalogue, I open it,
look at you, see your sister looking
at you, or past you. She cannot see the train.

2

Who's looking at you? The photographer has taken
a step back. Who's looking at you? Your mother
is looking at hands – your sister's. The echo of
her voice a moment ago: 'Show me your hands!'
You've got your hands behind your head, a touch
of bitterness remains, you're looking at
your sister – look at how she's holding out
her hands. They aren't dirty. Your mother looks
at them, holding out her left, not asking
to see yours. Who's looking at you? I'm looking
at your hands, the hands your mother isn't
looking at, the dirty ones, at shadows,
the platform, the tracks I can see because of the step
the photographer took, the lens, the frame, the page
that no one's looking out of for the train.

3

Who's looking at you? You stretch. Your sister stares
across the tracks, her back to you, her arms
are folded, I cannot see her hands. Your hands
are still behind your head, your palms are pressed
together. What's your sister want? To know
why your mother didn't want to look
at your hands. Who's looking at you? You stretch,
keep your hands to yourself. What do you know?
You know the bitterness that's on your palms.
You know the heat of waiting on a platform.
But do you know that you've been framed, framed
and painted and framed, by shadow, by the camera,
by the photographer, by the painter, and then
by me? And now there's someone reading this,
looking at you, still waiting for the train.

Long Enough

Under her hat, her eyes flatter all my dreams.
Red as her lips, the hat offers nothing more.
    If I just look at her long enough,
    I'll remember what I once was looking for.

Chasing a ball, a boy runs across the sand.
Walking along, a man also crooks his knee.
    If I just look at them long enough,
    I'll remember what they wanted to tell me.

So little time, remarked the librarian.
So many books, he said, making up my head.
    If I just look at him long enough,
    I'll remember what I someday must have read.

Two painted boys playing flute and a guitar.
Though they're just paint, I can hear the melody.
    If I just look at them long enough,
    I'll remember what they wanted to tell me.

Schism

Every fifteen minutes,
the quarter hour rings
from one church tower,
then again, seconds
later, from the other.

Pale Horse

I have seen the palest horse
coming round the bend.
Its hoofbeats echo closer
as I near my end.

O, is there a light,
a light that shines for me,
to guide me on the darkest ride,
on the longest journey?

Here comes the palest horse
saddled up and ready to go.
Now I must take me away;
where, I just don't know.

O, is there a light
at the end of the day,
to guide me on the darkest ride?
Will it show me the way?

Green Man

In memory of Sylvia Zysset (1971–2004)

She craned her neck to see the highest reaches
of the cathedral, where the Green Men loomed
in half-lit crannies, each a mason's dream
concealed for centuries by candle soot,
by the sheer height of Christian vaults and beams.

I strain my neck in vain for what she glimpsed
as passing clouds made sunlight ebb and flow.
Oh how her eyes once glittered when she chanced
to spot the Green Man on a book I own.
Around his eyes, the gilded leaves still dance.

Tambourine

Osip Mandelstam (1891–1938)

The walls are thin, with mildewed paper.
The sleepers sleep, but no one dreams.
The heavy air is short of breath,
and Osip plays his tambourine.

Pigeons dog the mongrels' steps
and coo at every window screen.
Goldfinches hide in wicker baskets,
and Osip plays his tambourine.

Car doors slam in every street,
unseen parts of one machine.
The elevators start to rise,
and Osip plays his tambourine.

The man who never goes to bed
forges being out of seeming,
engineering human souls
while Osip plays his tambourine.

Someone's drinking cherry brandy
underneath the hagberry tree.
Someone else is signing orders
while Osip plays the tambourine.

The cots, the blankets, and the cold
set the lice and typhus free.
Wooden nametags on bare toes
let no one play the tambourine.

Even the coldest winters end,
summer's gold puts out spring's green.
The Soviets are gone, but still
Osip plays his tambourine.

Blackbird

It was before the light began to change
words into birds. The eyes of the cunning
man, somebody who called himself
nobody, followed the circling gulls,
and he knew he would leave again.
Taking a boat, but no companions,
he made his way to the mainland,
the second time he'd left it all behind.

Arriving at an empty stretch of sand,
he beached the boat far from the water,
shouldered one oar, and turned his back
on the waves. The journey took much longer
than an aimless journey should. Then deep
in a forest far from any he'd ever known,
a man with eyes unlike his own demanded,
'What is that fashioned thing you're carrying?'

But Nobody could not explain the sea,
and when he tried out 'river' on this man
who'd never seen more than spring or stream, the light
in the leaves made a blackbird of the word.
The man cut off the branch it landed on
and asked to be shown a river. The stream
kept to their right as they headed toward
the sea. The water widened with his eyes.

With 'river' clear, the blackbird disappeared.
They cut more branches from the last tree
in which it had sung, and made themselves
a raft, another word for the man to learn,
a kingfisher that flew with them until
the sea became a swift sailing over
every cliff and house and wall
across the wastes of water, far from home.

Without A Lyre

for Brigitte Oleschinski

Every book contains broken traces
of each of its readers, remembering remnants beached,
still breathing, between Scylla and Charybdis.

But now I'm on the *Argo* as Orphea
challenges the sirens without a lyre,
her spoken words her only instrument.

Louisiana

Around the corner is a rusty gate
cursing in a gust of April wind.
A sudden hailstorm bursts across the street,
sounding out a greeting on the ground.

The fountain babbles on about the past.
Graffiti thunders in the sun-drenched square.
The pigeons bob around the picnickers,
pick up their morsels, and pursue the sparrows.

Down to the towpath, twelve uneven steps.
On the wobbly dock, two wooden benches.
The single bell that rings to call the ferry.
Four tousled ducks expecting some old bread.

The gutted mansion blazed a dozen times
before it was devoured by the ground.
The music of the summer never ceased,
but crickets are the only singers now.

The air grows thicker with the rising heat.
Swans don't bless the water anymore.
The weathervanes bemoan the willful wind,
while flags and awnings thrum redundant chords.

Just as a broken traffic light turns yellow,
and then red, but never, ever green,
a sailboat races on the littered sand.

The breeze fills nothing where the sail should be.

A butterfly blows in the motel window,
meanders slowly to the bedside table,
and settles on the printed butterfly
on the lamp's forsaken Chinese shade.

A roadside animal stares down the lights,
its retinas just colour passing by.
Warm asphalt calls it to its life or death;
the chestnut beckons from the other side.

Beside the Interstate, Othello speaks
his last soliloquy to nobody.
Four lightning storms encircle the horizon,
engulf his purgatory, drown his pleas.

The porch swing's silent; on the faded cushion,
a snake is coiled in the windless noon.
It flicks its tongue to catch whatever smell
is rising from the clapboards into blue.

Ars Conjectandi

Festschrift for my father on his seventieth birthday

Invito patre sidera verso. (Jakob Bernoulli)

Halfway up the stairway's supple curve,
Jakob turned and saw his father's stare,
baffled and angry, pursuing his every step.
Those pebble eyes had bought and sold so much;
the family business deftly hovered in
that searching face. It wanted now to sell him
into the ministry, the goal of all
his parents' yearnings, which had risen before
the cold, indifferent sun on the vacant morning
of this petulant child's guileless birth.

'Kepler', Jakob said, 'made mathematics
into honest money by measuring
the volumes of many different casks of wine
to make the vintners fair. All raffish tipplers
and fine-tongued connoisseurs owe him their thanks.'
He did not mention Johannes' true vocation:
the mastery of planetary motion
through equal areas in equal times.
Just so would Jakob study the visible stars,
not the vagaries of haunted heavens.

His hand was damp against the banister.
He heard his father's every breath and felt
his own fall into step with it. That gaze
fixed him as if he were a star, despite
the unbent certainty of his defiance.
His feet grew heavy; his mind began to follow
invisible ellipses beneath the pressure
of that steady eye. And there they stood
until his father turned away without a word
and left his son to dry his sweating palms.

His thoughts described a logarithmic spiral,
the selfsame curve of infinite renewal
he was later to define, and desire
for his gravestone, the pattern followed by
the growth of many snail and mollusk shells.
Inside his opaque vertigo, his eyes
pursued the bending horns of the gazelle,
the phyllotaxis of the cones of spruce
and pine, the distribution of the seeds
in flowers. The order of the leaves was his.

He turned to climb the stairs, but stopped. His fingers
fumbled damply at the back of his neck
to undo his fine-linked golden necklace.
One end in each emboldened hand, it formed
another curve he one day would explore,
the catenary of suspended chains.
He swung it gently back and forth and took
one step, then more, on that familiar stair,
the metal pressing deep into the skin
of his still-moist thumbs and index fingers.

The biblical Joseph ascended the seventy stairs
of Pharaoh's throne and spoke a different tongue
at every step, all languages unknown
to that supplicant before. And half
way up, he stopped and laughed, his outrageous joy
contagious to the Pharaoh. Just so did Jakob
ascend, hands outstretched, the necklace swinging,
each step more strange and certain, each to him
like Joseph's wondrous words and laughter, each
anticipating theorems yet unproven.

Halfway up the stairs, I turned to say
that I would not pursue Bernoulli with you;
that prosody, not probability,

would be my study. Did you turn away?
You laughed, but not, at first, contagiously.
I was the one who turned without a word.
But now I've found my seventy tongues in lines
mastering imaginary motion
and equal areas in equal verses
that spiral ever on, like Jakob's joy.

Flugelhorn

Tom Harrell, 'Autumn Picture'
Basel, 29 April 1996

Bars before
the end, lowering
his horn, one note

fading, he bows
his head, leaving
four trio chords,

sustained, descending,
accompanying
the music of nothing.

Thomas Hardy Listens To Louis Armstrong

So little cause for carolings
Of such ecstatic sound
– 'The Darkling Thrush'

Looking out across the winter lawn
at trees he knew were there but could not see
for mist, he listened to the gramophone

a younger friend had brought to play him shellacs
purchased on a trip to America.
His hearing was not what it once had been

when he fiddled with the bands and sang
in churches all around the county,
but still those strains came trilling to

his infirm ears, which he'd insisted
were unable and unready to hear, to *hear*,
this brazen song, full-hearted, taking up

caresome things and making them carefree.
Did he care for these ecstatic tunes?
Did he sense that this was more

than a ditty of its time? As if all time
were the trumpeter's, Gabriel's gift,
insistent calls beyond the calls of bells,

keeping him dreaming like an unseen tree.
He sat there, leaning on his cane like a picture
hung and covered in a hall, like an old man

in his darkening study at the end
of a day, the end of the song, the end
of another year, and tried to hear.

How the trumpet blew, drowned out
the winter wind as he dreamed on,
somnolent, unaware, to this song

with an under-echo of what he'd played
at fairs and weddings, for the dancers
and the dance, unnoting, unwitting, unwrit.

Verses

He scratched a few more words into the desk.
The wood resisted only for a moment.
The paper lay before him, blank as ever.
There's always something one would like to hide.
Once more he read the note she'd passed to him.
What should he make of her uneven hand?
She sat so still, just looking out the window.
Her verses did what verses mean to do.

Notes

'Monk's Dream'
The Brad Mehldau Trio's version of Thelonious Monk's
'Monk's Dream' appears on *Live at the Village Vanguard: The Art
of the Trio, Volume Two* (1998).

'The Last D'Athée's Complaint'
The Magna Carta, clause 50: 'We will entirely remove from
their bailiwicks, the relations of Gerard of Athee (so that in
future they shall have no bailiwick in England) ...'

'There'
Line 3 puts a line from Talking Heads' 'Heaven' (*Fear of Music*,
1979) into the past tense.
The quotation in lines 5 and 6 is from 'Shafty," from Phish's
The Story of the Ghost (1998).

'Your Mileage May Vary'
The italicized lines are from a wide range of songs that I grew
up with.

'The Circle Maker'
The story of Honi the Circle Maker can be found in the
Talmud.

'The Morning after the Night Before'
Radiohead, 'There There', from their album *Hail to the Thief*
(2003). But the singer here is Nadia Leonti.

'Grateful Dead Concert'
Yes, Deadheads, the last line is a mondegreen.

'Long Enough'
Vermeer's 'Girl with a Red Hat'; François-Marie Banier's
photograph of Samuel Beckett on the beach in Tangiers;
Arcimboldo's 'The Librarian'; an apparently imaginary

painting by Frans Hals (perhaps based on 'Two Boys Singing').

'Pale Horse'
Paradise Lost, X: 590.

'Tambourine'
This poem is based on an anecdote in Ralph Dutli's
Mandelstam. Meine Zeit, mein Tier. Eine Biografie (Zurich, 2003).

'Flugelhorn'
The band accompanying Tom Harrell at that show: Don
Braden (saxophone); Kenny Werner (piano); Larry Grenadier
(bass); Billy Hart (drums).

'Thomas Hardy Listens to Louis Armstrong'
Hardy died in 1929; Armstrong's *Hot Fives and Hot Sevens* were
recorded between 1925 and 1929.

Acknowledgements

Many thanks to the editors of the following journals for publishing some of these poems:

Cross Connect; *Eyewear*; *Hobble Creek Review*; *Horizon Review*; *Laurel Review*; *Leviathan Quarterly*; *Light Quarterly*; *Literary Imagination*; *New York Sun*; *Nth Position*; *Orbis*; *Other Poetry*; *Peregrine*; *Poetry*; *Poetry International*; *The Reader*; *Smiths Knoll*; *Softblow*; *Stand*; *Staple*

'He Who Hesitates' was set to music by Nadia Leonti and released on her band Leonti's CD *Everyone/I* (Faze Records, 2009). 'The Morning after the Night Before' was also set to music by Nadia and released as 'It's Alright' on the Leonti CD *Pink Maria* (Irascible, 2013).

'Land without Nightingales', 'Sundowning', 'Better Never Than Late', 'The Morning after the Night Before', 'Spring in My Step', 'Long Enough', and 'Pale Horse' were set to music by Andrew Shields and appeared on the CD *Somebody's Hometown* by his band Human Shields.

'Thomas Hardy Listens to Louis Armstrong', 'The Seven-Year-Old Atheist', 'Final Exam', 'Edge', and 'Spring in My Step' appeared in the *Poetry Calendar* published by Alhambra in Belgium in the years 2006 and 2008 to 2011 respectively.

'Aftermath', 'Flugelhorn', and 'Schism' appeared in the chapbook *Cabinet d'Amateur*, with German translations by Ulrike Draesner and photographs by Claudio Moser, as volume two of the series *Kunst zu Texten*, edited by Dieter M. Gräf and published by Darling Publications (Cologne, Germany, 2005).

Thanks

Thanks to my teachers: Barney Tanner, John Daniel, Denise
Levertov, Daniel Hoffman, John Felstiner, Al Filreis, James
Longenbach, Stéphane Moses, and Karl Pestalozzi.

Thanks to my friends and fellow poets: Geoff Brock, Padraig
Rooney, Donald Brown, Andreas Mauz, Durs Grünbein,
Ulrike Draesner, Dieter M. Gräf, Rob A. Mackenzie,
Michael Hulse, Katy Evans-Bush, Jill Alexander Essbaum,
and everyone who 'gathered together on this Thin Raft'
in Basel.

Thanks to my musical collaborators: Paul Baer, Markus
Bachmann, and the members of Petting Zoo, Onomatopoeia,
Psychic Sidekicks, Human Shields, The bianca Story, and
Leonti (especially Nadia).

Thanks to Todd Swift, Edwin Smet, and everyone at
Eyewear, and thanks to Benno Hunziker for the photos.

And most of all thanks to my families: PDSR & DEJ
and SLAM.

EYEWEAR PUBLISHING

EYEWEAR POETRY

MORGAN HARLOW MIDWEST RITUAL BURNING
KATE NOAKES CAPE TOWN
RICHARD LAMBERT NIGHT JOURNEY
SIMON JARVIS EIGHTEEN POEMS
ELSPETH SMITH DANGEROUS CAKES
CALEB KLACES BOTTLED AIR
GEORGE ELLIOTT CLARKE ILLICIT SONNETS
HANS VAN DE WAARSENBURG THE PAST IS NEVER DEAD
DAVID SHOOK OUR OBSIDIAN TONGUES
BARBARA MARSH TO THE BONEYARD
MARIELA GRIFFOR THE PSYCHIATRIST
DON SHARE UNION
SHEILA HILLIER HOTEL MOONMILK
FLOYD SKLOOT CLOSE READING
PENNY BOXALL SHIP OF THE LINE
MANDY KAHN MATH, HEAVEN, TIME
MARION MCCREADY TREE LANGUAGE
RUFO QUINTAVALLE WEATHER DERIVATIVES
SJ FOWLER THE ROTTWEILER'S GUIDE TO THE DOG OWNER
TEDI LÓPEZ MILLS DEATH ON RUA AUGUSTA
AGNIESZKA STUDZINSKA WHAT THINGS ARE
JEMMA BORG THE ILLUMINATED WORLD
KEIRAN GODDARD FOR THE CHORUS
COLETTE SENSIER SKINLESS
BENNO BARNARD A PUBLIC WOMAN
ANDREW SHIELDS THOMAS HARDY LISTENS TO LOUIS ARMSTRONG
JAN OWEN THE OFFHAND ANGEL
A.K. BLAKEMORE HUMBERT SUMMER
SEAN SINGER HONEY & SMOKE
RUTH STACEY QUEEN, JEWEL, MISTRESS

EYEWEAR PROSE

SUMIA SUKKAR THE BOY FROM ALEPPO WHO PAINTED THE WAR
ALFRED CORN MIRANDA'S BOOK

EYEWEAR LITERARY CRITICISM

MARK FORD THIS DIALOGUE OF ONE - WINNER OF THE 2015 PEGASUS AWARD
FOR POETRY CRITICISM FROM THE POETRY FOUNDATION (CHICAGO, USA).